POEMS TO A KING
Can I Get You
H!gh

A COLLECTION OF POETRY

AND UNSPOKEN WORDS BY A. Iverson

THIS IS DEDICATED TO ME. BECAUSE AT SOME
POINT AND TIME I LOST WHO I WAS. BUT
GAINED WHO I NEEDED TO BE-

I Love You-

CONTENTS

1 Nature v. Nurture   Pg. 1

2 Delightful Illusions   Pg. 28

3 The Alchemist   Pg. 52

4 Kintsugi   Pg. 71

Poems to a King: Can I Get You H!gh is a collection of poems and self notes full of High Thoughts and Magic Trips. From Nature, to the Universe and the Sea, a little whimsical, but it's truth.

This book of poetry is written as a reminder that you truly are a Divine Being.

Divided into four chapters, experience a trip filled with raw emotions exposing the journey of growth, sexuality and duality, self-discovery and empowerment.

NATURE
vs.
NURTURE

If this World

If this world were mine
I'd make you a King
Black as night
But as colorful as the day

I'll teach you the secrets
Of conquering this being

Immortal King!

Just know they'll try to snatch your
crown
They'll tell the world
One of the homies
Shot you down
They'll make an example out of you
Put your body on display
They'll throw dirt on your name

But we will forever
Scream out
Long Live the
King!

Long Live the Great!

If this world were mine
I'd give you every day
Sunny
Crenshaw Blue Skies
To take the Pain away!

-TMC

Dear black man

Dear Black Man,
I Love thee
You are everything
A King should be

Don't let your ego destroy you
You can overcome any battle
If you put your mind in tune

And I will be right next to you
Protecting your heart
Feeding your mind
Building you up

Loving You

XoXo
The Black Woman
aka
Queen

Knowledge is Power

Can you make my panties wet.
With your intellect?

Can you make me cum
To your conversation?

Bringing me higher
into your vibrations

Make me climax
To the stroke of your tongue
As you tell me about the galaxies
You want to take me

Exchanging your energy
With me

I'll have you up all night
Learning more and more

About this synergy
This inner peace

My Inner G

Are you the type of guy
That will let me ride his
Mind?

Deeper conversations
I want you tell me
All about your greatest fears

Open me up
So I can expose my
Truth to you

Leave me dripping
For more and more
As you expose

Your

Knowledge

Duality Part I

I struggle with duality
Living in this reality
I struggle with the physical
And spiritual realms
that holds my truths

Creating a world only I know

I believe in good and Bad
And I love to be Good
But
Bad can be Good too

I struggle with duality
Feeling the pulling and pushing
Of uncertainties

Half woman
Half man
A King
A Queen
A Dual Being

Little Girls

Dear King,

Little girls need fathers
To teach them
How men should be

So be an example of
The man you
Would want
Your little girl
to believe in

<u>Boyz II Men</u>

They never see the tears of the
Heartbroken.
Cause their tears were
stolen like a thief in the night
They were told to be quite
Little boys don't cry

But those little boys
Grow to be men
Who don't really know
How to deal with Tragedy
and unforgiving Sins

So to hide the pain

They find themselves
in between the legs of lovers

Young girls who are
conditioned to be

Mothers

Taught that a man is a companion
Needed for survival and protection

But how does a woman raise
a boy to be a man?
When she was never taught
how a man should be a man

Who has the blueprint
For the little boys who
were told not to cry
dry your eyes and man up?

But!

What is being a man
If he can't express
How he feels within

A conditioned cycle
Everyone is playing pretend

Lesson learned.

You can't spend on others what they aren't
willing to spend on themselves.
-Self Note 2017

Flower child

Flower child
Let me grow wild
Let me grow free
From the roots
To the crown
This flower blooms
Wild and Free

The Suns' Flower

I told him to call me Sunflower
The prettiest flower you could ever see
Yea she's the prettiest flower that
could ever be

Because she gives great life

She stands tall and firm
She grows strong
Waving in the winds
Bending but never breaking
Continuing to grow
stronger and taller

Have you ever been to
a sunflower patch?

Do you know how tall
a sunflower can grow?

See she is the prettiest
flower of the bunch

But often goes unnoticed
Due to the rose that
Grew from the concrete

But this sunflower
Grows wild and free

She brings great light and energy
She is powered by the SUN
That's why he named her after he

A SUN in a FLOWER

She brings light to your world
She brings life to your world

So when you see a Sunflower
Do not pick her
She is not to be plucked
From the roots of where she stands

But when you see a Sunflower
You stand right next to her
You nurture her
and watch as she continues to grow

And feeds your soul
Give peace to the Sunflower
The one that grows so wild and free
Just let her live

She will be everything you need

I'm ok

I'm Okay
That's what her mouth says
But underneath it all
There's a fire burning
In the pit of her stomach

It's like thousands of fireflies
Decided to take flight
Lighting up her insides

She wants to tell you
How she feels
But she can't find the words
She doesn't no where to start

So she tells you "I'm ok"
With the hopes that you can
Read her mind

She wants you to
Douse the pain away
She wants to communicate

But "I'm ok"
Will have to do today

Afraid of the Dark

Don't be afraid of the dark
That's where beauty grows
Like the coal buried
deep under ground
A diamond is created
When beauty finds pressure

De-flowered

I fell in love
When he ran his fingers
down my spine

The soft feel of him
He was reeling me in

He wrapped his fingers
around my neck
And as he licked his lips
I knew how this would all end

He called me Beautiful
Right before he plucked me
I guess that was his way in

He chose me over all
the other flowers
Now that may be his biggest sin!

He took my flower
Held the sweet scent between his nose
He savored my goodness
He knows I'm way better than a rose

Plant me in your soil
And I'll fertilize your mind
I am a deep-rooted creature
There's no going back this time

Do you know who I am sir?
I think you may have me confused

I am the one who sacrifices
Eternal sunshine
Just so you might have light

I am the one with stars in her face
And an unwavering taste for Sunrays
Magic, and Raindrops

Did you know I create life?
I feed your soul
And if you are bold
I might let you take
a handful of my Seeds
Just so you might eat

But don't devour me
Save your energy
We both know
This can't last long

Because a Sunflower
Unearthed
Withers and weeps
But will forever
Linger on your mind

Lover

I am the lover you needed
Because I found the lover
I needed in me

Cause & Affect

You keep telling yourself you are
exactly where you need to be. And this
is the truth. Each time you tell
yourself this you are faced with
situations that can make or break you
in some kind of way. The more you tell
yourself you're where you need to be
the more you begin to unlock the pieces to
the puzzle. Your journey is not for
everyone so stop trying to share it
with people who don't care. It's ok you
don't have to feel any kind of way
about it. Everyone is on their own
journey marked with trials and
tribulations and each and every one of
us infect and affect each other in some
way. You realized how you infect others
good and bad. You choose what you will
allow yourself to do and what you will
allow others to do to you. Remember
you are NOT a victim of your
situation.—Self Note 2015

Bare

I wanted to bare my soul
Open up my chest
And give you the one organ
That allows me to keep
ticking

I wanted to bare my pain
Opening up my brain
Sharing my vulnerability
Just so that you could
understand the
rain

I wanted to bare my love
Engulfing your spirit like a hug
Wrapping my love around your neck
Holding on tight. It's suffocating

But it's as real as it gets

I wanted to give you all of me
Pieces of myself
I gave to you
Not expecting anything
In return

I realized that somewhere in that time

I died
I was the very thing I despised
Someone so in love
They don't realize
Love was not given

It was not reciprocated
It is not unconditional

But conditionally
False
A pretender

My imagination ran wild
Because I thought you felt
The same way as me

I internalized my light
Just so I could brighten
Up your life

Baring everything
But receiving nothing
From the other side

That's the Way Love Goes.

   As I sit here and think. At what point
in this journey did I lose love along the
way. I remember as a kid I associated love
with the butterflies that flutter through
your stomach when you talked to your
crush. Love was something I knew nothing
about but wanted to feel. Where do you get
love? Can I pick this shit up in a bottle?
Is it a prescriptions only a doctor can
prescribe?

   I thought love was. Late night phone
calls and early morning text. Love was the
smile you get on your face when they walk
in the room. Or when someone says his or
her name. Love was the unexplainable
silence when you're around them because
you get speechless by their presence. Love
was unconditional with no real definition
and no real origin yet people fight for it
every day.

   I thought love was giving your all to
someone even if they only gave you pieces.
But this wasn't real love. This Love was
for show. You show people you love them. I
remember the first time I said the words I
love you. The sound rang through my head
and echoed off the walls. It made me feel
grown up. That's what they told each other
right? But I had no idea how to show that
love.

How do you know WE love? Is it by the words we speak? Is it the actions we display? Or is it a little mixture of everything and some more shit in between. Is love pain and fear? Or is love happiness and action.

Can the two be intertwined like the connection of the umbilical cord to the baby and the mother? Do we need one to feed the other? How do we find love? Love definitely isn't found late night creepin'.

We find love in the simplest of places. Love is found between people who discovered they never really knew what love was. Love is found when you stop looking for it in others and find it in yourself. Love is reconnecting old thoughts and old memories. Preparing to take on the world together. Love is honest when it is spoken from the lips.

Love is captivated in the energy you bring. Love is found when given the chance to completely be yourself around those that matter. Love is traveling with nothing but a suitcase and a journey we cannot see. Love is accepting my flaws, making me open up and showing me love still exist in a world of lost people with hate in their hearts. Love is displayed and others take notice. With you I wear love on my sleeve so the whole world can see. Because you are Me! - Self Note 2015

Butterfly

I hope this reaches you in time
So that you understand that
My love was intended to
Make you grow

That my dark side
As over bearing as it is

It was created to show you
That when light
Reaches your heart
You become light from
The inside

I hope this reaches you
As you move through
This world

Don't allow the negativity
To bring you down
But use it as a stepping
Stone
To fly to new heights

I hope this reaches you
I hope you learn to reach
for new destinations
Higher realms of love

No matter how hard it may get
You will grow

Just think
The caterpillar
Goes through excruciating pain
Just to be a butterfly

And the flowers growth is
marked by Beauty
Pain and
Sacrifice

Say it twice
"I Love Myself!
I Love Myself!

The love of self
Is my Sacrifice

The Love of self
Is the preservation of Love"

Knowing you can withstand anything
And you will be stronger

So I hope this reaches you

I hope you realize
The only thing you need in this life

Is love of self
And
Time
to heal the pain

Dear king

I gave you my attention.
I poured bravery down your throat
and this is how you repay me?

You leave me broken hearted.
Stranded and confused.
As if I didn't tell you what to do?
I told you I needed you
I told you I loved you.

So why was that not good enough?

They say actions speak louder than
words.

Maybe that's where we found our
disconnect.
No actions just throwing words around
That we thought sounded great.

So you ripped my heart out my chest.
Dropped it on the cold concrete
pavement.

Heart stolen,

Heart broken
into pieces.

But King I'm not mad at you.

It's me that should have known.
I can't expect to receive love
without SHOWING you how it's done

Summertime Flowers

I've spent time in darkness
Deep down
Grounded in the secrets of my thoughts
Drowned by sorrows and worries
Believing here I stand
Defeated and fallen

Then I opened my eyes
I finally see the light
It's been surrounding me
Blinding me to the point
I could only see what I wanted see
But I'm focused now

Something happened when I fell
I realized that all along I was growing
Sprouting from the ground
A new flower has been born
And she is wild
And carefree

Unapologetically
A Queen

DELIGHTFUL
ILLUSIONS

Serial Lover.

I feel like I've been down this road before
it's all too familiar and I'm trying t figure
out why I keep turning down the same road.
There really wasn't an expectation for what
has been happening.
Well actually if I'm being honest there was!
And maybe that's the problem.
I keep having an expectation of finding love.

I want real love Unconditional and
everlasting love. And in many ways whenever I
come across someone I instantly begin to think
maybe this one is it. I try to enter
situations with an open heart and mind. But
maybe that's what makes me naive to what's
really going on.
I believe real love knows what it is before
the interaction even begins. I have to stop
romanticizing about situations and scenarios
only I see.

The reality is most people aren't even
prepared or ready for that kind of self-less
love.
I deserve all of the beautiful magic I
create in my life. I deserve to surround
myself with people, places and things that
remind me that Love is truly the gift I've
been searching for. I am open to receive and
I'm a more than willing to give.
I just hope that the person that is supposed
to be here recognizes all of the possibilities
and understands I am everything I say I am-
and everything you might think of me to be.
Self Note 2018

Skin Deep

This is dedicated to the soul
The one
Who takes control

Inside this being

You continue
To remind me
That everything
I need
Is truly

Skin deep…

Magic Trips

Do you believe in Magic?

Stories of casting
Spells and potions

Speaking words
And putting
Things in motion

Magic to heal
The spirit within

Speaking words ·
Over your life

Magic
Fills
You
With
Light

Universal Love

Take me to a Universe
Only we can get to

Tell me I'm beautiful
Tell me I'm smart

Tell me I can have your heart

Love at 2am

You got that 2am kind of love
That shhhh!
Don't tell nobody that
we fucked kind of love

And all I want to do is drop
Love down your throat.

Let love coat your insides.
Filling you up with all
the desires of your mind.

I want to take love and
wrap it around you.
Reminding you that no matter
Where you go I'm right beside you

I am the rib God took from you.
Created just for you.
I know you feel it.

Love created deeper meanings when
We decided that's what we were giving.

So I'll never be afraid to tell you

I love you!

I love you because you are
in fact me!
A true spirit
A connected soul in
2 beings

Let it Go

You have to let it go!
As much of a lover you are and all you want to do is give and receive genuine love. Stop wasting your time and energy on guys who continue to take from you. They don't appreciate what's in front of them but you have to honor what you are presenting. It's time to focus on you. Just like my momma said.

All my intentions are on manifesting selling your script, picking up some creative writing gigs and enjoying your freedom. Focus is the name of the game. It all ends today! You have to get right for you. Put your order in. And you want it your way. Your imagination works for you here. Anything you can think of big or small can happen today if you really truly believe- Self Note 2018

Smoke

Like a blanket of smoke you cover me
Curled up between my lips
Lingering like sweet kisses
I inhale your goodness
Filling my body with colors of love

You get me High

I was baptized in your love
            Taken to the sky
Now I'm the one that's high

            This whole time
    I thought I was in control

            But to my surprise
I was the one who didn't know

            I stopped smoking weed
                Just so If could
                            See

                    How high
            You really get me

Acid Trips

Your lips remind me
of acid trips
Sweet and full of color

Psychedelic colors
surround you

Once I let your taste
dissolve on my tongue
I knew I was in for
a wild run

Giggles

Your energy fills me with
laughing gas

Dancing to the hues of you
I'm thankful to experience
Such a trip

Acid strips
Everything down
To where it needs to be

Exposing my real
Feelings
Exposing your true
Meaning

L$D

Lies sold dreams
I took the first hit
And I couldn't help
but believe
You gave me hope
You told me to trust
And have faith

Never did I think that
this could be
fake
From that moment
I was on a wild goose chase

You filled me up
Hallucination of really attaining
All the things I've ever dreamed

Your Lies Sold Dreams
I took a hit of your LSD

It took me high
through the
Crystal lined sky

Kaleidoscopic colors
Dance around you and I

You opened my mind
You opened my eyes

Relieving my anxiety
Dancing and
Staying up all night

You cleared my thoughts
Hand in hand we walked
towards dancing colors
Lost on this acid trip

Your Lies sold dreams

Delightful Illusions

I know that this isn't right
I saw this in my dreams at night
A place for lovers like us to
Escape

<u>OD</u>

greetings from the other side

i got too high

overdosed on your drug

i didn't mean to die

i thought i could handle your supply

what a surprise

your drugs were all lies

<u>Self-Infliction</u>

Self inflicted wounds
They are like my battle scars

I knew exactly what
I was getting myself into

But instead of listening to
the voice in my head
I followed my heart

So now that I'm all
bloody and bruised
I figured this is the perfect
time to choose
Choose who I want to be
Walk down the path that
is paved just for me

No longer will I let the
wounds of my battles
Scar
me for life

No matter where I might fall
I will get back up again

Because the battle
is not lost and
the war has just begun

Part I

There is peace
There is clarity
There is Love
There is happiness
There is Beauty
In the moment

Flaws

I have flaws
Not sure how to
Embrace them all

Imperfect perfections
I've been too afraid to share them
To embrace

This space
I'm in

Deep down I know
its the insecurities
That put the fear in me
I look in the mirror
I like what I see
But that's not me
It's skin deep

It's inside the being

It's the voice in my head
That says I can't make it
The attitude I get when
I'm tired of fakin'
The depression I feel
When I succumb to feelings
That aren't even real

Insecurities run havoc on my dreams

They're like monsters
Chasing me in my sleep

I wake up in cold sweats
That's that anxiety

It's trying to kill me
Heart beating faster
The monsters turn up
In my day dreams

They just don't want to
Let me be

The want me to scream
They want me
To give up
But I'm to damn stubborn
To take a knee
I know in reality I have
Everything I need
I can't let the insecurities
Get in the way of my dreams

So I stop running
To confront the monsters
Chasing me

Face to face
I embrace
Every part of me
These things make me
Me
Good or bad

Because once you
Realize
Things aren't
What they seem
Life is really but a dream

Can you feel me?

I write poetry
Because it makes my heart feel free
It awakens my soul
Reminds
Me I am
Free

Anything I write
It can really happen for me
So I set my intentions right

Sharing a space
To divide
The person
And the soul

I just want to be able
To express

Get a couple things
Off my chest

And hopefully someone
Out there can feel it

<u>High Thoughts</u>

Sometimes poetry doesn't make sense
It's like that time you got high
But you weren't sure if you were high
So you start explaining
all the things you
Would normally do if you were high

Then you stopped

And realized

Maybe
I'm
High

Third Eye

My third eye has been watching you
Centered in the middle
She forms thoughts of you
My third eye creates
tunnel visions of you
She wants to see the
good amongst the
bad in you

Sat you in the middle of her room
She reads you well
She knows what you're thinking
She knows what you said

My third eye is watching you
Waiting for the day
you are awaken from
the haze

My third eye is seeking the day you
realize
That our eyes were supposed to meet

Connecting
Manifesting

Can I get you High?

Do you mind if I get you high
High out your mind
High off my vibe
Tantalizing your thoughts
Where we stop time

Can I take you high above the sky?
Into a realm made just for you and I

I want to bring you into my world
Surrounded by stars and galaxies
Sharing our deepest thoughts and
memories
Learning the true meaning of
Synchronicity

Pouring into one another
Surfing on our frequencies
Dancing colors
Creating thunder

I frequently think about
Exchanging our energies

Our Heart beats in tandem
As you inhale
Take me up
Fill your lungs
And I will exhale love

So do you mind if I get you high
I promise I won't bite
And once you get that first taste
You'll know that this is a high
You want to chase

<u>Reflections in the mirror</u>

I looked at myself in the mirror for the first time in a long time. Like really LOOKED. Who is this person standing before me? I really don't recognize who I've become.

Having to learn to love yourself again is probably one of the hardest things to do. To really accept yourself for who you are can be a challenge if you're not paying attention to the changes.

It was hard to see myself changing physically and mentally without even trying. It has forced me to see myself for who I really am. And to accept the fact that I may not have actually loved myself they way I needed to before.

I have the opportunity to learn to love everything about me as I watch myself transition into the person I know I'm supposed to be.-Self Note 2015

Have you seen the Master Peace?

I'm gonna paint pictures
With my words
For the people that
Never heard of me

Creating clarity
Just so you know
I'm a masterpiece
I'll show you how
I mastered Peace

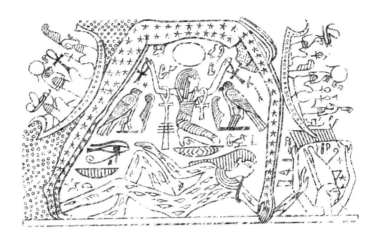

THE
ALCHEMIST

Dear Self,
Get out of the FUCKING way

Courage

What does courage mean to you?

Is it making sacrifices
for the greater good?

Facing a challenge or a fear?

Doing what others may see as
impossible?

Is courage confidence? Or does
confidence come before courage?
I want to challenge myself to be
courageous. I want to step outside
of what is comfortable. I think
when you put yourself in positions
where you have to challenge
yourself you learn
what it takes to be courageous. But you
also learn to do things without fear.

We tell ourselves we can't do things
even when we don't try them. We scare
ourselves out of being told NO or
failing that we don't even try our luck
with a possible YES or SUCCESS. I feel
that with people, especially black
folks, we tend to allow others
perceptions to influence US.
Even if at the beginning
you know for sure it's what you want.

Just because it was hard for them
doesn't mean it's going to be for you.
And even if it is that's okay because
you'll get through it. Things are only
hard if you don't try.

There's an abundance of resources,
Networks and opportunities
for us to take on challenges and come
out winning!

I want to be successful but I keep
Asking myself how? How am I going to
get there? I'm searching for the
answers but I feel that it's
staring me in the face I just
don't see the big picture yet.-2015

SuperBeings

Did you know you are royalty?

People stolen from their homeland.

They were true Kings and Queens!

They survived all the torture
that they were put through.

And somewhere down the line
You came to be.

Descendants of
SuperBeings!

Before the day ends!

Dear Black Girl,

We love you! You are appreciated and
needed. You are enough just the way you
are. Continue to live in black
excellence Believe in abundance!
And Live a Lavish &Luxurious Life
Because you deserve it

Fire

I feel like fire
Burning from the inside out
Burning everything I touch
Scorching the pavement as I walk

I spit fire from my tongue
Watching my words
Ignite my path

I feel like fire when
things don't go my way

I AM Fire

Cleansing and pure
Igniting a hot fiery
inferno only I can get through

<u>Light</u>

When you look at me
What do you see?
A little girl
Drifting in the sea
Of her own uncertainty?

Do you see the stars?
as they encompass
her whole being

Illuminating the darkest
Parts for the whole
World to see

Ode To Decisions

I decided today will
be the last day

The last day of tears
The last day of fears
The last day of dealing
with Bullshit!

I decided today was
going to be the
Last day
The last day that I give
you pieces of me
and My Energy
I can't get back

The last day I let you
Penetrate my space

I decide that today was
Going to be the
Last day

The last day of trying to please you
The last day of trying to help you
The last day of trying
to share something

With you that is not
going to be reciprocated

Because I AM WORTH IT!
I decided that my value
has gone up
And the price has gone up
It has doubled and tripled

I decided today was the last day
That anything I have is for sale
You have to get this whole price
Or you can't get it at all

I decided that today is
the last day
That I compromise myself for you
Or anybody else that doesn't
Truly give a Fuck about me

Today is the last day
That I give my energy
And my peace
To people
Places
And things that truly
Does not matter
I decided

What about you?

Infinity

I am in a position of
Receiving
In an ever evolving cycle of
Giving

<u>Real Eyez</u>

Real Eyes, Realize, Real Lies
So if eye cut you off
Don't be offended
I'm just trying to protect
My energy
From enemies

Clearing
Negativity
Out my mind
Out my space

Realize these eyes
Have cried thousands of tears
But shedding tears

Reminds me
I'm still alive

Dear King

I want you to know that
love doesn't have to be found
amongst the crowd of people
But if you allow yourself
to sit in the silence
Love will find its way to you.

Moon-light

I want to be like the moon
Strong and bright
She illuminates the night
A constant reminder
That even in the dark
There is
Light

The Journey to Happiness

People (Black People) never suggest
being apart of the arts. It seems like
everyone in our society (Black People)
looks at the arts, as something that has
no meaning and it's impossible to get
into. Which pushes the narrative that it
holds no monetary value. It's sad to see
that many kids are taught to push their
creativity aside to pursue more "realistic
and well paying jobs". It's even sadder to
think that most of these children are
those that look like me.

As I continue to discover what
direction in life I want to take.
Everything around me is pointing towards
Art and Culture.

I'm not really sure exactly what it
means. I don't want to be afraid of the
unknown. This is a different challenge for
myself. And I'm excited for what could be.
I'm excited for the lesson learned and for
the experience I'll collect on the
journey. My pursuit of happiness hasn't
ended. I think I've been blind sided by
other things that I forgot that I am on a
journey and the things that I think are
causing unnecessary road blocks are just a
part of the story.
Stick with the Journey-Los Angeles, CA
2015

<u>Smoking Words</u>

I call this smoking words because
I smoke these words
No I wrote these words
No I toke these words
I blow these words
Inhale and exhale

Giving you all of me
Sharing my thoughts and my
Deepest insecurities
I decided I would much
rather you see
Me! See me for who I am!

I smoke my words
Because it comes easy
Sharing them like it's 420

Most people find it easier
For you to fake with them
But just like a hard toke
from the smoke
You just might get choked
Pretending To be someone you're not

No need to create another
image of me
Always wore my heart on my sleeve
Because it's to much energy
Trying to keep up with
the pretend me
So I just chill
Giving you real

Smoke!

<u>Possessed</u>

I hope one day you realize

Everything you say you are

And everything you want to do

Can be achieved
If you believe

But to believe you have
to be so possessed by the belief that
Nothing
No one
Not even Yourself
Can get in the way

Duality Part II

I struggle with duality
Sometimes I'm not sure
if I'm a man
Or if I just have
a strong personality
Most times I like to get piped
But sometimes you can
call me a dyke
See I like what I like

A strong king to hold me
tight at night
A pretty queen
That knows how to
Touch me right

Embracing love from two souls
I don't want to have to choose
This is where love grows

Duality is real
So don't tell me how to feel

Dear Queen

Dear Queen
The Crown is heavy
But you
Are *Strong*
The Throne is high
But you
Are *Mighty*

XoXo
A Queen

KINTSUGI

- THE ONCE-BROKEN VESSELS ARE MADE WHOLE.

What is Broken?

What if I told you
that nothing is ever really broken
That we can put our pieces back
together and be whole again

Im-Perfection in our on view
Because we allowed ourselves to be
consumed by the flaws
that tried to make us fall

But instead we picked
up the pieces

One by one
Taping them and
filling ourselves up with gold
Nuggets of knowledge to protect us

We become something new
We become whole

Not like before
but pieces of that
Reshaping ourselves to fit
this new mold

Never be afraid to be
consumed by the darkness

Never be afraid to
be broken down
or
left
Broken hearted

Because nothing is ever really broken.

<u>Life Jackets Save, I don't</u>

I catapulted out of your love today

Once I hit the deep blue sea
I did a backstroke just to get away

Don't tell me that you love me today
Those words sound sickening
when you say it that way

Don't try to jump in after me

Don't expect me to save you
I can't be pulled down
Drifting into the lost depths
of your Atlantis

I no longer can be your life jacket
You have to learn to swim on your own

Float
Coast

Whatever you need to do
You can make it on your own

I'll be right next to you
Cheering you on!

Rain Showers

Rain showers and love poems
Keeps this dancing heart
Better equipped
To handle any situation
Life may come up with

I AM Perfect

I'm perfect
Imperfect
Perfection

I'm perfect in myself
can't you see it?
I shine through the cracks of the
broken pieces
Put back together again by love

I picked broken up from the floor.
Putting them back together
like pieces to the puzzle

Like cracks through the soil,
that's where the soul grows

Like the roots to the
flowers and the trees
The cracks help me breathe

I collect food
and quench my thirst
So you can say that
these cracks nurture me

Perfection
Divided into im-perfect pieces

So I say I am-Perfect
Putting my pieces
back together
to make
Perfect
whole
again

At Your Best, You are Loved

The Universe keeps making a call. Are you going to pick up? It's calling you to your purpose. It has prepared you to take control of your throne. Are you ready to answer the call or are you to scared to achieve greatness. I've been taking wins and losses trying to help people on this race while still trying to help my self.

I allowed my self to be covered in darkness, covered in pain, anxiety and depression. Covered in past traumas and conflict. Taking on other people's demons and issues. I stripped myself of all the things I thought I knew, wanted, had and believed in.

I broke myself down to pieces.
Scattered myself across the country.
Prepared to be put back together again. I
have been called everything under the SUN.
Allowing words to infect my soul.

I had to realize it's not what they
call you it's what you answer to.

I chose to only respond to those that
address me with Light, Love and Peace in
their Hearts.

I have been giving too much of me for
free. And finally the price has gone up.
Because that myth of being priceless will
have you fucked up. Surrounding myself
with people who understand their fight in
this life and are ready to take the stage.
I know my worth. I know I am worthy of
everything I ask for.

If you're not prepared to receive what
is rightfully yours what are you truly
living for?

<u>Wet Dream Music</u>

I wake up to wet dreams about you
Soaking wet sheets
I want to be fucked real good from
behind
Sweat creeping down my spine
I'm not sure if it's yours or mine.

Touch me
Suck me

Make my body feel like there's
no where else to go
You are eternally
etched in spaces
only love can grow

We have eternalized our souls

The cadence
The rhythm
We rock the boat

We make love that's as good as
Rock and roll

The Great Shift

I'm Shifting
I'm drifting
I'm pulling away
Today was the final day
As the rain pours down
And it washes
Everything away
I am reborn
And Renewed

Reminded
That Yes! dry eyes
Can see the sky
But it's after the rain
That brings all of the love
And washes the pain away

As your tear drops fall
And It mixes with the ocean
Allowing you to float onward
Believe in yourself
And your dreams
You will flow to them
The waves will bring you to
Anything and everything you
Desire

Float On

I'm somewhere in the
middle of the ocean
Floating
Allowing the ocean
To pull me in with

Its currents
I'm flowing
Carrying me to
Destinations unknown
But somewhere far away

I had to escape
I had to get away

Leaving behind
All the things
I've known

I had to go
I had to grow

I ran miles until
I hit the water
Backstroke
Breaststroke
Anything to take
Me further

But I got tired
I realized the harder I swam
The further back I'd go

So now
I just float
I ended up

In the middle of the ocean
right here in this moment

I decided to let go
And just float
Let the currents
Take me to the places
I should go

Surrendering all
In the middle
Of the oceans
With the sharks and their prey

I pray

I give thanks
Protected by
The Sunrays

Illuminated lights
Reflect on the ocean
From the sky
I know I'm
Protected by the most high

So I flow
With the go
Taking my soul
On the wildest
Ride ever known

The ocean is home

Part II

There is beauty in the silence
There is beauty in the wait
There is beauty in the uncertainty
There is beauty in this day

There is beauty in this life
So simple and so true

There is beauty in love
There is beauty in Me and You

Poem about Nothing

Pain can't live here anymore
Rain has been replaced by the sunshine

I shine bright
The stars decided
to align just right

No longer needing your permission
I do what I want

I pray to my God!
Giving everyday
Thanks

Because
I've made it a long way

I am living in my truth
Filled with my wealth

I have an abundance of riches
Dropping knowledge from my lips
Like sweet chocolate kisses

I fear nothing
Because "nothing"
Has no meaning

Has no action
Has no life

<u>R e m i n i s c e</u>

I smell you like the day
Fresh and bright
With a slight spritz of honey dew

I hold my breath
Making sure every bit of it
Flows through my body

I want you here forever
Being reminded of you
Everywhere I go

You remind me of a fairytale
The kid in me loves to dream
A hopeless romantic
But I know everything isn't
What it seems

I pray one day
We meet again

Sharing love and laughter
Journeys and downfalls
I look for the day
I see your smile again
And you take me in your arms
Holding me tight

And this time
Never letting go
We light the night sky
Filled with fireflies

Kintsugi

What keeps you up at night? The thoughts run through my head trying to find an escape that's not there.

I'm searching and looking hoping to find the right piece to the puzzle that will unlock the next step. But instead I'm still here. Searching this empty room looking for that same peace of mind.

When you realize you've been chasing butterflies in an open field you see they're harder to catch. Chasing ideas in a room full of silence. I'm trying to figure out what's next and my thoughts still remain the same.

I gather my thoughts. I expose my broken pieces to be put back together again. But there is no reconstruction for the broken because you will never be fully back together with those pieces.

You learn you have to create something new with the pieces you are left with. Fixing you with pieces of gold. That's the definition of a Masterpiece!

Peace

    Peace
    To Pieces
    of ME
    I was too afraid to show

The Queen

If only you knew of
the places I've been

The faces I've seen
The hurt that it caused me
You would then only get
just a glimpse of the Queen
that stands before thee

Skin so gold
Eyes so brown
My crown grows to fit
Growing stronger each day
I've been through a lot of shit

But King I like it this way
Gives us something to talk about
When we finally decide to give
our love a chance!
Until then I'll keep a smile on my face

Because I am Queen

On Repeat

This is dedicated to him
You told me to write a poem for you
So this I what I thought of

Frequently your frequencies
Pass by and visit me
Your energy it speaks to me

It tells me stories
Of love and synchronicities
They remind me why we are
meant to be

I yearn for the days
I wake up next to you
Telling you about my dreams
As you kiss me on my forehead
And you tell me I can have anything

Love and loyalty
That's all we really need
But I don't want it just for me
I want us to believe
Believe that our love
Can last for an eternity

I'm glad for the day we met
It felt like my love
for you was instant

You did magic for me
Casting a spell on my heart

I didn't have to be high
To know that you were a drug
And I needed the supply

For some reason you made me feel
Everything about you was real

From the coils of your hair
To the curl of your smile
You made my heart run a thousand miles

Your touch felt like everything
A strong black man
Your mind reminds me
Of shooting stars in the galaxy

I will treat you like a King
Gladly put down my armor
So that you can love me
I'll surrender it all
If you're willing to protect me
Like your Queen

So I hope one day I get
to express my love
To shower you with
everything you deserve

Just be sure that it is returned

Like an everlasting circle
Or maybe a poem you forever want to
read
Or a love song on
Repeat.

Message to the king
Remember we trust you with our lives
We love you!

About the Author

A.Iverson is a Counselor turned Creative
Writer and Entertainment Entrepreneur. She
is a proud alumnus of The Great Bethune-
Cookman University in Daytona Beach, FL
and Full Sail University in Winter Park,
FL. She found her love for writing at an
early age as a way to escape her own mind
and her ever-changing environment. She
finds inspiration in the people, places
and memories she's gathered on her
journey.

P.S

You Smell like weed.

Made in the USA
Columbia, SC
25 March 2025

55661014R00062